UNCAGED

A Book On Changing Your Mind

By William Baker

This book does not guarantee monetary or actual results but it does allow for an individual to breach the boundaries of their mind that can lead them to several aspects of what success may entail to them.

This book is dedicated to everyone who has been there for me in every way, even through my recycling of friends. To my family, I love you, thank you.

To Mary: Thank you for being everything that I couldn't be. Through all the dark times and bright ones, you're my rock, my one and only. I love you.

To my daughter, Alexis: Please let this serve as a reminder that you can do anything in this world that you put your mind to. I love you, kiddo.

INTRODUCTION:
Tell Yourself The Truth

Telling yourself the truth is one of the hardest things a person can do in their lifetime. It takes a certain amount of courage to say, "This is my fault that I'm here." Whether you're in a good or bad spot, setting religion and beliefs aside, there's very little in this world that you cannot control. You got to that good or bad spot because you put yourself there. Very rarely will we come across an individual who was able to find their way with preset items such as money, family owned company, and whatever else, but they still have to work to maintain and be consistent.

Be honest with yourself. For me, I had to be honest and stop being such a narcissistic prick. I had to stop blaming everyone else for the position I was in. It definitely took a few years to learn that. Failed relationships, failed friendships, and even failed opportunities led me to this point right now. It isn't about controlling what's happening around you, it's about how you react to it. How do you react? You tell the truth to yourself. Being able to tell yourself the truth also shows that you respect yourself. I can tell you right now, I had VERY little respect not only for folks around me, but for myself.

This part is the HARDEST mental barrier that you will cross. If you can get through this, then the rest of the barriers will seem like jelly. I can PROMISE you that if you can just admit the truth, your journey will take you to places you never thought possible.

Lastly, the best practice you can do with this is starting. 80% of success is starting in the first place. It may take you a day, it may take you years, but the whole point is, you can't start tearing that wall down until you build up the courage to pick up the sledgehammer. In fact, go pick it up, I dare you.

PART 1: COMPLETE THE TASKS

Part of being successful in your own way and having your mind uncaged is to complete your tasks. Completing something as simple as making your bed all the way up to cleaning your house can have such a positive effect on your mind.

Let us take a look at your morning routine. When do you get up? What do you accomplish in the time you're awake? Are you a late riser who prefers to rush off to work with no plan to the day or are you a habitual planner to the point that nothing really gets done (aka analysis paralysis)? Either way, you have to start with a morning routine. Having your routine teaches you a level of discipline and opens your mind up to the ability to manage your time better and accomplish more throughout the day.

I'm sure that everyone, at some point, has used the phrase, "There's just not enough time in the day!" As they scroll through social media or watch television. Now, I'm not saying no one should enjoy these privileges but at some point, you have to ask yourself, "With the time it takes for me to find something on television or scroll through social media, what could I be accomplishing?" Some folks might not have that desire and that is perfectly okay, but, if your goal is to succeed in what you put your mind to, making the decision to let those go for a while until you accomplish those tasks can truly benefit one's path and dream.

Success looks different for everyone, but all success stories have something in common: CONSISTENCY. Personally, for me, success was finding myself and who I was as a person and incorporating that into my everyday routine. You don't have to have a million dollars, own a bunch of land or properties, or have all of the luxury items one would assume a successful person would have, but merely a sense of happiness is considered the greatest success there is. What did I do to achieve that? Below, I'll give you my routine. You can use it exactly or you could tailor it to fit you:

430am: Wake up, pre-workout, take out dog(s)
500am: Gym/workout at home

600am: breakfast and plan my day
(If there's extra time due to a shorter workout, I read!)

Everything after that was dependent on when appointments were, where they were located, and so on (I'm in sales). It took a while to get use to it because I had to go against what I call my lazy brain, but eventually, it became habit and now it's a part of my routine. Of course, there are days where it changes up or I take some time off but one thing still remains the same: I'm still getting up at 430am every day, without question.

"Even on your days off of work?"

The answer is YES! Do it when no one else wants to!

"How is a morning routine (or even an evening routine) going to affect my mindset?"

Great question! It absolutely can! Accomplishing these tasks before some people are even awake gives you the rest of the day! If you work long hours, then get up earlier or go to bed later. There's no magic potion to this and there's no pill that can cure laziness, you just have to do it. That leads me to the next task at hand: Motivation and Luck do not exist.

PART 2:
MOTIVATION & LUCK DON'T EXIST

Yes, you heard that right, motivation and luck are things that I believe don't exist. To some of you, if not most or all of you, you've used that infamous phrase, "I'm just not motivated." Or "I'm very motivated today!" To understand this, let us take a dive into each of those words and what they mean so I can explain their non-existence thoroughly and tell you what I replaced those words with.

Before I give definitions, here is my perspective on understanding these words.

Let's say you meet your friend out for dinner one evening. You were supposed to meet them the evening before but you had a doctor's appointment.

"Where were you yesterday? They ask.

"I was at the hospital." You reply.

"Oh my goodness, are you okay!?" They gasp.

"Oh yeah, it was just a follow up appointment from the previous visit." You reassuringly respond.

My point in this, is there's a negative connotation that is attached with going to the hospital. Yeah, sure, the fact someone goes to a hospital as a follow up but in some cases, it is true, but the overall point is, why does there have to be something wrong? Your friend just go put through an emotional ringer in a thirty-second time span.

All of our words have meaning and being a writer, words are important to me, especially in the context in which you use them. It seems contradictory to me to use a word like "motivation" that is supposed to have a positive connotation attached to it and have it be used as something negative.

MOTIVATION

The definition of motivation based on a quick look up via Google:

mo*ti*va*tion
Noun
"The reason or reasons one has for acting or behaving in a particular way"
"The general desire or willingness of someone to do something"

So my question, when I read this one day, was why would we use a fancy word to justify laziness when we could just say that we did or didn't want to accomplish something? What have the ramification been when we mask the TRUTH of what we have done, good and bad? Why would we manufacture a sense of okay-ness and allow ourselves to slip into the cycle of our own mediocrity? When I say mediocrity, I mean why would we put ourselves in the position we always complain about being in? It just doesn't make any sense to me.

So how did I change that? I, instead, use the word "inspiration." Inspiration SOUNDS more uplifting and positive, thus, impacting my thought process. It is so easy to mask something negative with something neutral, but again, until you come to terms with yourself and tell yourself the truth, you'll have a hard to getting through the initial steps of changing.

LUCK

Luck
Noun
"Success or failure apparently brought by chance rather than through one's own actions"

Personally, I think luck is a derogatory term that devalues one's successes in an effort to level their failures with those successes. There are so many cases where I will see on social media that someone comments on a person who posted a picture on vacation and they say,
"You're so lucky!"
Not to sound too "soft" but, that person worked their ass off to be

able to take that vacation, whether by themselves or with their family.

There's not too much in this world that you can't control so how can one be lucky for rewarding themselves (or accept a reward) for their hard work? For a more down to earth perspective, that's like complaining about a 10 year old getting a piece of candy for doing extra chores and you didn't get one although you chose not to do the extra chores. How does that make any sense? It doesn't.

Here's a better suggestion: clap for your friends even when it isn't your turn to be rewarded.

So, instead of using the word luck, I replaced it with result. How can this be used in an example? I'll show you:

"The result of your hard word has to be an amazing experience for you (and your family)!"

A result is a direct correlation of what we have put in, good and bad. What will your result be? It doesn't have to be extravagant but it could be something small like getting a good grade on your paper.

Results become apparent when opportunity meets preparedness. If you're not prepared with a good mindset (and whatever else), then how you will obtain the result you desire from said opportunity?

So, I implore you to attempt to replace the words motivation and luck with inspiration and opportunity. Why do I push this so hard? Here is why:

THE RICE EXPERIMENT

Place 1 cup of cooked rice into two separate containers and place a lid on them. Write on one container "Thank You Rice" and on the other, "Stupid Rice." Place them in your kitchen approximately 12 inches apart. Once a day, or more if you'd like, go into the kitchen and up to the respective containers and say "Thank You Rice" and "Stupid Rice." Make sure to be genuine (even though it seems silly) in your thank you by coming from a place of gratitude and in your stupid from a place of anger and frustration. The result will probably, no, in fact, blow your mind.

The "Thank You Rice" through approximately 3 weeks, will show very little, if any, aging, while the

"Stupid Rice" will have more liquid, mold, and smell worse.

The moral of that example is positive words with good intentions will nurture and encourage growth while negative words with negative emotions will rot and destroy you. This is the same as having that friend that always complains and is always negative. Don't lie, we've all had or have one.

This isn't some voodoo, witchcraft thing, but it's backed scientifically that being positive vs negative will have different effects. Don't believe me, then try it for yourself.

Make sure to be kind to yourself and others. Our mindsets are extremely important and we have to treat them as if they're a muscle in our bodies.

PART 3: CAPACITY VS ABILITY

This part is a part that some might find difficult, especially due to temptation, social peer pressure, and letting emotional decisions overrule logical ones. The reason it is difficult is because we, as humans, tend to prioritize emotional values over logical decisions, even if it puts us in a bad position. Also, due to certain pressures from society and our peers, things like always having the newest and best product all the way to always wanting to have everything, it can drive some individuals to make irrational, impulsive decisions. Some of that is due to the same levels of dopamine that get released as if one was to be doing something they love and some of it is due to just not thinking before acting. Let's use the car reference to translate this.

To define, CAPACITY is the maximum amount that something can contain. Your ability to make decisions based on the knowledge and experience you possess, in this instance, defines the boundaries of capacity. In other words, if you can't, whether at fault to you or no one at all, coherently and comprehensively navigate through a decision on if you have the capacity (the understanding) to handle this new burden, then you should probably consult a trusting professional or friend to help guide you prior to making such a decision.

Let's say you got a good paying job, making more money than

you've ever had before when you were living paycheck to paycheck.

Those who don't understand financial literacy, they will start living a lifestyle without understanding its limitations and the risks and consequences that come with it, but will also not have the greatest living conditions or are behind on other bills but ignore them. Spending the money on themselves because it makes them feel good, is a real thing, but also an issue. Is there anything wrong with making yourself feel good? Absolutely not, but there is a limit to this.

So, you go and purchases a new vehicle, increasing your monthly payment to four-hundred dollars a month from two-hundred a month, because you like the attention through reactions off of social media and envisioning the future of showing your friends and family.

In this instance, just because you have the ABILITY to purchase the vehicle, doesn't mean you have the CAPACITY.

For ABILITY, just reverse the scenario:

If you didn't have room in your already stretched budget and purchasing the vehicle puts you in the negative, and you buy it anyways, knowing the consequences of doing so, then you shouldn't get it (barring exigent circumstances). So, this means that just because you have the CAPACITY, doesn't mean you have the ABILITY. All of this is just a scenario of course that isn't situationally specific for anything other than information and understanding.

Some may ask, "Well, how can I remedy this issue?"

To start with capacity, start learning your limitations, both comprehensively as well as physically, if necessary. Learn on how you can develop your capacity through learning and resource management. Just keep expanding your knowledge, you'll retain more than you think.

For ability, think of it more along the lines of opportunity. When you get an opportunity, you have to decide, based on your capacity, if you're capable of handling it.

All of this wrapping up, they go hand in hand, especially when it comes to understanding what you read previously as well as what the next step is: Decision vs Sacrifice.

PART 4: DECISION VS SACRIFICE

We have all said to others that we have sacrificed something in order for another opportunity, or the one you're currently in, to take hold. In the game of chess, one would potentially sacrifice their pawn in order to move into checkmate status against their opponent; however, there could be a greater perspective to this: you KNOW that you are needing the pawn to go down to win, so you made a DECISION to do so. You could argue that they both seem to be the same thing, but as I mentioned before, perspective and words are everything. Allow me to explain.

DECISIONS

Decisions are empowering and based on logic. When we make a decision, sometimes we will write out the pros and cons and research each side to weigh out the opportunities and make an educated decision.

To me, there's never a maybe in my vocabulary anymore, it's either yes or no. That's what a decision is to me. If I'm not required to give an answer right away, I will wait, in applicable situations, until I can make an educated decision. So, in other words, making a decision is black and white. Very little to no emotion is involved because, just like in chess where the only emotion is the player, a logical decision must be made with each move of every piece.

Chess is a game where you must make calculated moves and think three to five steps ahead of your opponent. In the game of life, you will have moments where an opportunity presents itself and you are ready for it, but also moments where that same opportunity comes and you aren't ready for it.

Regardless of which one it is, you will have to make a decision with the information you have. In the first instance, you can be calculated and direct, already knowing what was coming. In the second instance, you have to switch your priority from knowing to reacting. What do I mean?

When we come across those situations where we are limited on information, we instead have to switch our mindset from being prepared to being reactive. We have to be just as calculated with our reaction and more malleable so we can make the best with what comes at us. In these situations, it is very easy to become engulfed with the notion that we SHOULD have been prepared or start complaining that it happened when we weren't ready, but guess what? That's life, get over it.

Regardless if you're ready or not, making a decision is crucial. Going back to the beginning with telling yourself the truth for a moment: if you skip that step and get here, making a decision will be much harder, if you even make one at all. Do yourself a favor and if that is you right now, skip this and go back to the beginning and start over.

SACRIFICE

Making a sacrifice sounds so much like a negative experience to me. If you received an amazing opportunity to travel the world and be monetarily rewarded but you think of "sacrificing" time with your friends, you're convincing yourself to not do it because of how said friends would view you. At that point, you're willing to limit your exposure to your dreams in an effort to prove loyalty and nobility to those friends. A year down the road, you'll think about where you're at then and be disappointed in your progress when you previously had the opportunity. That is called regret. So, in essence, when you view your decisions as a sacrifice, you're allowing the door to stay open for regret to make a home, which regret will remind you that it is there, whether a day or year from then.

It also leads to resentment. When you and your significant other make a sacrifice to take a vacation, knowing funds are tight but you want to have fun and feel like rewarding yourself, if that significant other really wants to go and begs you to and you do it, only to get home and realize you have no money. Some people wouldn't bring up the issue. Your significant other will talk about how much fun they had while your brain is stuck on the aspect of spending too much money. Not only are you regretting that sacrifice, but you're also harboring resentment for your partner, even though it isn't their fault that you didn't communicate. In this instance, when you communicate beforehand, logically instead of emotionally, all of that information can be reviewed objectively and without recourse and you can then DECIDE to hold off on that vacation until you both are ready.

I make decisions, not sacrifices. I'll give you an example of the hardest decision I've ever had to make in my life. This is a full transparency portion.

It was early spring of 2024 (not too long ago) and I had received the news from my wife (now ex-wife) that she had been seeing someone at her work for a couple months. It devastated me because without reason or justification, my trust was broken and ripped into a million pieces.

For two to three weeks, I was lost but I still had to work, I still had to be a dad, I still had to live. I had to make a decision: I could be sad and do nothing or I could be sad and get to work. So, I was sad and got to work. Some of us unfortunately know the side effects of what adultery does to one's view of themself. It's a tragic and horrible feeling of worthlessness BUT, there's an opportunity inside of all of it that I found. It wasn't just that I was moving on from something destructive and debilitating, but merely the fact that I was MOVING. I was progressing, whether it was just getting up and making my bed in the morning to doing a good job at work.

I started my routine back again, hitting the gym, eating better, really trying to switch my mindset from "Am I good enough?" to "I'm fucking good enough." There were days where I was close to breaking down in the gym and days where I let the rage take over, but I was dealing with it in a healthy way. I was getting better and when I tell you the physical changes made a difference in my body, it also made one in my mindset. I could think clearly, see my future, and above all, I could be ME.

Fast forward to the end of June/ early July of 2024, I wasn't looking for anyone or anything, just continuing my progress. My close friend of 3 years, Mary, messaged me saying she was on tour (she's a photographer) with a band and would be coming to North Carolina (lives in Pennsylvania) and invited me and my bandmate, Nick, out to the show. So, we went and it was an absolute blast. Mary mentioned that she was visiting a friend near where I was living as well, which was awesome! Long story short, we ended up hanging out several times over that weekend and thoroughly enjoyed each others company.

After a couple weeks of "deliberation" and view on optics with kids and how it could work living eight hours apart, we decided to become a couple.

Fast forward to the end of August, we were in talks of making plans on the next five years, since that was when my daughter would be graduating high school. Then, an opportunity struck.

I was discussing the potentiality of what careers were up there and her close friend's husband reached out with an opportunity to work for that particular company. I go all of the information I needed and quickly made a decision. It was a fantastic opportunity.

Then I asked, "When does training start?"

"It starts in 2 weeks. Can you do it?" He replied.

I though for a moment and the exact words not only came across my mind and came out of my mouth, "FUCK IT. Let's do it."

So I had two weeks to make plans, pack my house up, and move all the way up to Pennsylvania. What made me decide so quickly?

Part of it was my job at the time was going down the drain and becoming harder and harder to navigate and handle. The other part was I would be with Mary and her kids. Now, the hard decision was to leave my daughter behind with her mom. The school she is at is amazing and all of her friends were there, on top of a legal custody arrangement in place. Some of you may think of me as a bad parent but here is the perspective I offer:

Kids might be oblivious to their physical surroundings a lot of times, but they're always watching and always listening. I have raised my daughter to the best of my ability thus far and I can continue to do so through co-parenting efforts and logical, common sense.

I would rather my daughter know that I still show my efforts and have her see those efforts in her life and in mine, to teach the lesson that you can be successful and still fulfill your obligations as a person from a distance. I would rather deal with that and have her SEE that happiness than to watch me sit and be miserable. What if she sees that misery and assumes responsibility? I'd rather her not have to carry that burden.

The overall point with this section is you're going to come to a cross road where you'll have to make a decision and you need to think of it logically and not emotionally. Don't allow regret and resentment to settle in your heart.

PART 5:
SUCCESS IS NOT AN ACCIDENT BUT NEITHER IS FAILURE

Being successful can take on many different forms. Let's take music for example. The music industry is a lot smaller than most people think and everyone pretty much knows the next person. It is a tough business to not only get into, but to also be consistent in unless you have a large, experienced team.

Now, before I dwell on the different looks of success, it all starts with……you guessed it…..TELLING YOURSELF THE TRUTH! Personal accountability is important to hold in every step from beginning to end and if you skip that, it all just falls apart.

To me, success is defined as personal fulfillment versus societal standards. What I mean by that is, if you just want to be playing cover songs in your garage with your buddies and it makes you happy, then you're successful. If you want to tour the country and/or the world and enjoy the fame, then you're just as successful if you're happy.

The baseline in that is your happiness. Success is directly linked to your happiness. Regardless of where society thinks you're supposed to be or even your family and friends, if you're happy, then you're successful and that's all that matters. If anyone has a negative response to that, then they themselves are not happy with where they are at as a person.

When you set your goals to achieve the level of happiness you feel that you deserve, not only is having personal accountability important, but being responsible is just as, if not more, important. That is where "imposter syndrome" is located in all of this. If you're not responsible with your brain, your decisions, and your responsibility, you will find a way to self destruct. When that happens, you will retreat on everything you did up to this point and be back at square one or start digging your own hole. Don't let it get to that. Remember everything that you've done prior to this and use that as INSPIRATION to push forward.

I could fill an entire house with the amount of failures and lessons learned faster than some folks who would only fill up a room. Does that mean I'm a terrible person? Nope. Business owners and leaders fail constantly, they live for it, they strive for it. There's an ideal of being "perfect" but shoot for the stars and land on the moon. Be grateful with what you have.

Before I got all of this down, I was an awful person. I didn't care what happened as long as I got what I wanted. That kept landing me in the arms of frustration but I finally realized that the narcissistic approach that it was everyone else's fault wasn't going to get me to where I needed to be or wanted to be.

I live for the opportunity to say, "Hey, I messed up, that was wrong. How can I do this differently or make it right or better?"

There's nothing wrong with being scared to fail, but you shouldn't be scared to learn from that lesson. A lot of life is reacting to the consequences of your actions so, react appropriately and you'll see the results of what you wish extend far beyond the boundaries you though were possible.

PART 6: BE THE DUMBEST PERSON IN THE ROOM

We all have friends and family that we turn to in an effort to extract what we like to call an opinion, but in reality, we are looking for them to make that decision for us. Why is that? Based on my experience, it's because we don't want to bear the responsibility of the negative result. We want to give the negative credit to that friend or family member but take the credit for ourselves when it goes right. I understand being selfish, but why would we do that to those we love and admire? It just doesn't make any sense.

Is there anything wrong with asking for an opinion? Most definitely not! In fact, I encourage it! It's like making a pros and cons list but getting it from other people's perspective instead of just your own. The problem I have, is when we rely on these folks to make the choice for us based on influences they have. Why do I have that issue?

How many of your friends or family that you go to have been or are in the position that you wish to be? To ask in a better way, how many friends or family members do you know are happy with where they're at in life that have the position to be able to tell you their thoughts and you take that into logical consideration? Probably not many. If there are, bravo! You've done this next step: Surrounding yourself with those who are more "successful" than you are.

Being the 'dumbest' person in the room doesn't mean exactly what it says. You're intelligent in your own way! What this means is you should surround yourself with people who are "successful" in the area you wish to achieve goals. For example, if I'm a musician, having local musician friends in local bands can FEEL great and FEEL communal, but if your wish is to grow and tour and get well known, then make your circle full of folks who have toured or are touring. Now, that doesn't mean you should disown or never talk to your community or friends again, it just means you need to reallocate your time and efforts searching for advice from those who've never been there to those who currently are (or have been).

Does that mean your local community isn't intelligent or doesn't give sound advice? Most certainly not, but I'd prefer to take advice from someone or a group of people in a far more advanced position than me than those who are not.

In the field you wish to achieve ultimate happiness (or success), reach out to those folks already in that position. What's the worst they could do? Not respond? Say no? You're in no worse position than you were before you asked them, right? There's nothing wrong with getting 'shot down' but there's a positive: you tried. That's the hardest step! Eighty percent of success is showing up in the first place so, good job!

Those people you reach out to will most likely only spend their VALUABLE time on those who are serious for that change so, don't waste their time, just like you don't want yours wasted. Be respectful. After all, you're recycling your 'friends list' in an effort to maintain a successful or happy mindset, so don't just respect them, respect yourself. Respect their value and yours, too.

All of this brings up that last capitalized term: valuable. Your time is valuable and we have one life to live. How will you make the best out of it?

The ball is in your court now. Will you shoot your shot or will you just pass the ball and hope for the best?

Make your decision.

PART 7: BE CONSISTENT

This is the HARDEST part out of all of these steps: being consistent. Now that you've achieved what you've strived for, now it is about maintaining and improving things. It is very easy to get to this point and say, "Ahhhh! I've made it!" And then just stop. Wrong decision. Keep it going! Soon enough, those friends you stopped asking advice from will come to you and want the same thing and then it will be up to you to decide if you AND them are serious enough to spend your valuable time together.

There is a difference between consistency and intensity. Just because you do more, doesn't mean you're getting more work done. Think about that for just a moment and put it into perspective: Think of

consistency like a race: it's a
marathon, not a sprint. Don't gas
yourself in the first step or two in an
attempt to make up time or cut
corners and skip steps. Just trust the
process.

Part of being consistent is, as I
mentioned before, building your
habits, like a solid morning or
evening routine. A consistent work
out plan for the gym. A consistent
work pattern for your career.
Whatever it may be, build that habit.

The one thing I didn't mention
were setbacks. Everything can be
fine and dandy until one day,
everything SEEMINGLY just falls
apart, throwing you off of your
consistency. Now, this isn't written
to achieve perfection, I'm far from it
and frankly, there's no such thing.
This was written for YOU to

achieve the goals you wish to achieve by 'simply' changing your mindset and releasing your mind of negative thoughts.

When the setbacks occur, just remember, at that point, it isn't about how prepared you are, it's about how you react. Don't let it rock your mindset back to the beginning. Your mindset is stronger than you think. It may SEEM fragile, but it is most definitely strong. When it happens, also, find something positive that reminds you of why you're here, how you got here, and what you did to achieve that. Believe it or not, you're a lot further than you think you are now.

When setting your goals, make sure to challenge yourself but don't be unrealistic. For example, if you're wanting to lose weight, attempting to lose fifty pounds in three weeks is just unhealthy. Start lower, like say ten pounds every month (just as an example, I'm not a health expert), and as you achieve these goals, challenge to do more next time and celebrate the wins, no matter how small they may seem to be. If you don't hit ten pounds in a month but you hit seven, celebrate that seven pounds lost. At that point, you have probably already noticed a difference and you should be happy about that.

CLOSING ARGUMENTS

This journey is NOT for the weak but it will help develop your mindset to handle moments that could potentially make you feel weak. There's never a "right time" to start, just do it. Remember, decision, not sacrifice.

In an effort to summarize, let's put the pieces together with brief explanations:

1. Tell yourself the truth: be honest with WHY you are where you're currently at and be honest with being willing to put the time and effort into changing it.
2. Complete the tasks: with things like making your bed, accomplishing something daily can be helpful with changing and maintaining this new mindset.

3. Motivation and Luck don't exist: it's time to change your vocabulary - revisit the rice experiment
4. Capacity vs Ability: Just because you have the capacity to do something, doesn't mean you have the ability to do it and vice versa.
5. Decision vs Sacrifice: Don't let regret make a home by sacrificing (deciding with emotion). Let logic take regret and resentment out of the equation.
6. Success is not an accident but neither is failure: What you put into life is what you get out of it.
7. Be the dumbest person in the room: don't be afraid to surround yourself with people more

successful, or happier, than you. Learn from them.

8. Be consistent: just because you feel the change, doesn't mean you stop. KEEP GOING!

Overall, I want each and every one of you to know that however big or small your successes are, that I'm proud of you. I shouldn't be the only person in your life to tell you that but if I am, it is coming from a place of honor and great respect. I know how hard it is to get through life's mistreatment so, I'm with you.

I want to hear from you. I want you to reach out and tell me your story! Tell me the results of this book or if you've reached your goals and beyond prior to this, I want to hear about it. When we go through life, we do it together, good and bad.

About the Author

William Baker - William is a musician and writer in his late 30's. William has a beautiful daughter, Alexis, and always wants the best for everyone around him. He is originally from Oceanside, California, lived in Eastern North Carolina for most of his life, and currently resides with his wonderful and amazing partner, Mary, and 4 children in Pennsylvania.

www.ingramcontent.com/pod-product-compliance
Ingram Content Group UK Ltd.
Pitfield, Milton Keynes, MK11 3LW, UK
UKHW032334131224
452011UK00005B/72